DISCARD

animalsanimals

Cows

by **Renee C. Rebman**

Marshall Cavendish
Benchmark
New York

Thanks to Donald E. Moore III, associate director of animal care
at the Smithsonian Institution's National Zoo, for his expert reading of this manuscript.

Marshall Cavendish Benchmark
99 White Plains Road
Tarrytown, New York 10591-5502
www.marshallcavendish.us

Library of Congress Cataloging-in-Publication Data

Rebman, Renée C., 1961-
Cows / by Renee C. Rebman.
p. cm. — (Animals, animals)
Summary: "Provides comprehensive information on the anatomy, special
skills, habitats, and diet of cows"—Provided by publisher.
Includes index.
ISBN 978-0-7614-3977-6
1. Cows—Juvenile literature. I. Title. II. Series.
SF197.5.R43 2009
636.2—dc22
2008020906

Photo research by Joan Meisel

Cover photo: moodboard/Corbis

The photographs in this book are used by permission and through the courtesy of:
AP Images: 34. *Alamy*: Peter Cavanagh, 20; Duncan Usher, 24; Larry Lefever, 28; Agripicture Images, 30; Ulrich Faust, 36; Nigel Cattlin, 39. *Animals Animals - Earth Scenes*: John Stevenson, 25. Corbis: Richard T. Nowitz,15; Lester Lefkowitz, 17; Yann Arthus-Bertrand,18; Lothar Lenz, 27. *Getty Images*: Richard Price, 40. *Minden Pictures*: Heidi & Hans-Jurgen Koch, 1, 16. *North Wind Picture Archive*: 8, 10. *Peter Arnold Inc.*: Biosphoto/Heintz Jean-Christian, 4; PHONE Labat Jean-Michel, 7; S.J. Krasemann, 19. *Photo Researchers, Inc.*: Davis R. Frazier Photolibrary, Inc., 38; *SuperStock*: William Hamilton, 12; Rosemary Calvert, 22; age fotostock, 31.

Editor: Joy Bean
Publisher: Michelle Bisson
Art Director: Anahid Hamparian
Series Designer: Adam Mietlowski

Printed in Malaysia
1 3 5 6 4 2

Contents

1 A Noble History

A small *herd* of aurochs, the ancestors of the modern cow, *grazes* in the tall grass of an open field. Several females nibble on the tender green shoots while keeping watch over the younger animals. A large male aurochs lifts his head and looks toward the horizon. Its long, curved horns stand out distinctly against the blue of the sky. Suddenly, he bolts away at a swift run. The rest of the herd follows with thunderous hoof beats. Human shouts pierce the air. The hunters begin a chase but soon stop. Their chance for a kill is gone. The aurochs have escaped.

Aurochs were mighty beasts standing about 5 feet, 9 inches (175 centimeters), at the shoulder. The males

The zebu, a breed of cattle from India, is a direct descendant of the aurochs. Zebu can still be seen today in India.

weighed as much as 2,200 pounds (1 ton). They could be fierce fighters. About 2 million years ago, the first known aurochs lived in the region that became India. They eventually migrated to Asia and Europe. The zebu, an Indian *breed* of cattle, is directly related to the aurochs. The aurochs and the zebu were *domesticated* about eight to ten thousand years ago.

Aurochs are depicted in the famous cave paintings of Lascaux, France, which were created around 15,000 BCE In 1940, four curious teenagers discovered these paintings when they explored the caves. Of the two thousand images, nine hundred were of animals, including aurochs, horses, cattle, cats, birds, a bear, a rhinoceros, and a very distinct painting of a human. It is not known if the paintings were made to capture images of things important to prehistoric people or if the caves were used as a ceremonial place.

As people hunted aurochs, their numbers dwindled. At one time, the hunting of aurochs was restricted to members of royalty. In the 1300s, hunting was banned completely. The *species* never recovered, however. By 1620, the last male aurochs died in Poland. It is believed the last remaining female auroch also died in Poland in 1627.

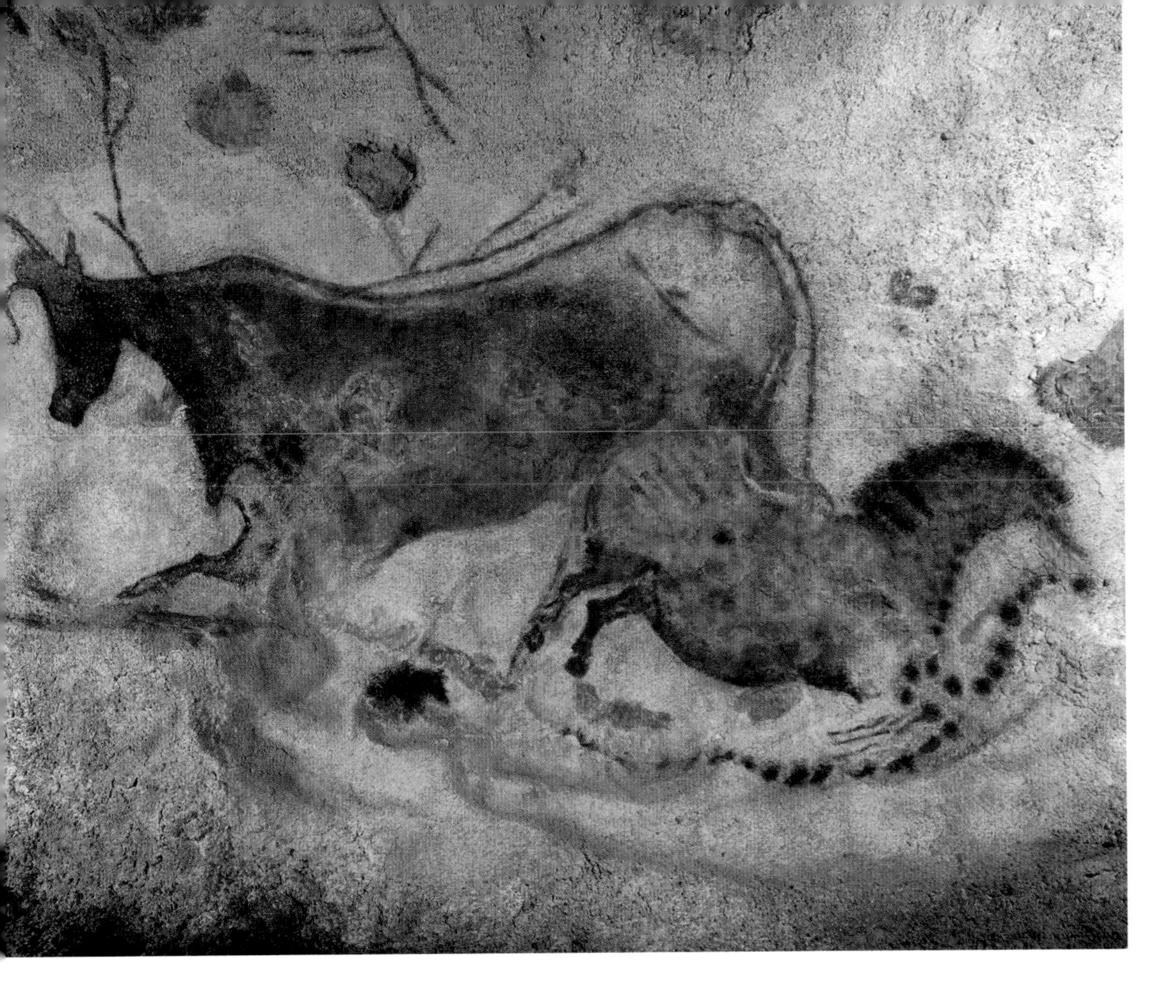

The cave paintings of Lascaux in France, are thousands of years old and show a number of different animals who lived during that time, including aurochs.

In 1493, explorer Christopher Columbus set out on his second voyage to the New World. His mission was to populate any lands he discovered and to claim them for Spain. He took seventeen ships and more than a thousand men to establish new colonies. Columbus also took cows and other animals to the Western Hemisphere. The Spaniards and their animals settled in many islands, including Puerto Rico, Guadeloupe, Hispaniola, and Cuba.

A family cow was kept by many families in the early 1800s.

In 1519, Hernando Cortez of Cuba sailed to Mexico. He was determined to take the land from the native peoples. Eleven shiploads of his men, known as conquistadors, landed on Mexico's gulf shore with cargo and animals—including cows. The conquistadors set up ranches with barns and acres of land for the cattle. They *branded* the cattle with a mark of three crosses. Some cattle escaped and roamed free. This is how cows eventually *migrated* to what is now the United States. They traveled through the lands that later became Texas and California.

Cows also made their way to the Americas on ships coming from eastern Europe. Thousands of *immigrants* moved to the eastern seaboard in the early 1800s in search of new opportunities. They sometimes took along the family cow, which provided important milk and cheese.

Civil War erupted in this country in 1861. Northern and Southern states fought over serious issues such as slavery. The war lasted four long years. Many farmers left their families to fight. With no one to care for them, herds of cattle roamed free, especially in areas west of the Mississippi River. After the

Did You Know . . .

Cows have shorter hair during the summer time. It grows longer in colder months. The Galloway cow from Scotland has long, shaggy hair all year because of the windy and cold environment they live in.

After the Civil War, cows were shipped to different areas by boat to start new ranches to meet the growing demand for millk and beef.

war, there were food shortages. People in the cities needed milk and beef.

For the first time in the United States, there was great demand for ranches to supply food on a large scale. A single family cow was not enough. Ranching became a necessity and a new business. Ranches were established in less populated areas and in much of the wild, unsettled West. Ranchers rounded up and branded the roaming cattle as they established their own herds. They sent milk, cheese, and beef to the East. The role of the cow became even more important in a country desperately trying to become whole after a devastating war.

2 All Shapes and Sizes

Cows come in various shapes and sizes. Some of their characteristics originated with the ancient aurochs. Two different descendants of this prehistoric animal eventually developed. One had a large hump on its upper back, while the other was humpless. The cows in the United States and other western countries have no hump. In eastern countries, cows have humps on their backs. The Brahman, an Asian breed, is a humped cow. Brahmans are hardy and can tolerate hot, humid weather. They can be found in a few areas of the southern United States.

A cow's most distinguishing features are large eyes, friendly faces, big *muzzle,* and rounded ears

Cows really do come in all shapes and sizes, including this Brahman cow, whose large hump on its back is its distinguishing feature.

that protrude sideways from its head. The cow has a heavy body supported by short, sturdy legs. All cows have long tails with a tasseled end that they flick to keep flies away. A cow's *udder* is located under its belly in front of its hind legs. This rounded sack with four *teats* is where the cow makes and stores milk.

Some cows have horns growing from the tops of their heads. These horns grow sideways, like their ears, and then curve upward at the end. Cows can use their horns to fight, but horns are not as necessary for modern cows as they were for their wild ancestors. In fact, many cows do not grow horns, or their horns have been removed. Cows with their horns removed are called polled cows.

Cows have nearly 360-degree panoramic vision. This means they can see objects at their sides, not just what is directly in front of them. Many light-colored breeds have dark circles around their eyes. Some experts believe the circles help keep flies away. Others think the circles reduce sun glare.

A cow's sense of smell is even better than its eyesight. Cows recognize their own calves by smell. They can identify more than sixty

Did You Know . . .

Wisconsin is known as the dairy state. It produces more cheese than any other state in the nation. Some residents of Wisconsin call themselves "cheeseheads" because of the pride they feel for their state.

This brown milk cow is one of the breeds which grow horns.

With its strong sense of smell, cows can easily sniff out their own calves.

individual cows in a herd by smell. They also recognize humans by smell—even people they have not seen for years.

While there are several dozens of breeds of cows, some of the best known are the dairy cows. There are six main breeds of dairy cows in the United States: Holstein, Ayrshire, Guernsey, Brown Swiss, Milking Shorthorn, and Jersey. 95 percent of all dairy cows are Holsteins, the most popular milking breed. There are about 9 million dairy cows in the United States.

The United States also has over 30 million beef cattle. Well-known beef breeds are the Angus, Hereford, and Shorthorn. The Angus is considered to produce the highest-quality beef. Texas has more beef cattle than any other state. It also has more farms—about 229,000. Alabama, in comparison, has only 23,000 beef farms. The famous Texan Longhorn

The Brown Swiss is a popular breed of dairy cow.

Species Chart

- Cows (females) usually weigh between 900 and 1,500 pounds (408 and 680 kilograms) and stand around 4 feet (1.2 meters) tall.
- Bulls (males) can stand over five 5 feet (1.5 m) tall and weigh over 2,000 pounds (900 kg). Size depends on the breed.
- One of the smallest breeds of cow in the world, the Dexter cow from Ireland, stands around 3 feet (1 m) tall and weighs less than 750 pounds (325 kg).

This Dexter cow, one of the smallest breeds, stands with its owners, who hold a trophy the Dexter won.

breed, known for its distinct appearance, can still be found, but ranchers keep it mostly as a hobby rather than for beef production. This breed was known and named for its long horns. The longest known set of this breed's horns spanned 9 feet (2.7 m).

The Texan Longhorn is easily recognized by the set of long horns on its head.

This bullock, a young male, is almost two years old.

Farmers and ranchers use cow-related terms in a more specific way than most people. Although cows are females and bulls are males, we often say "cow" to mean any cattle, regardless of gender. However, a cow is not technically a cow until she has had a calf. Before she has given birth she is known as a heifer. A young bull less than twenty months old is known as a bullock. A motherless calf is called a dogie. A suckler is a cow that is milking a calf. A cow that escapes being branded is known as a maverick. Finally, steer is the most common term for a bull that has been castrated. Steers have bigger muscles and produce more meat than bulls that can reproduce.

Cows are an important part of life in the United States and around the world. Their place in society has evolved from a single family milk cow to an invaluable asset in billion-dollar industries.

3 The Life Cycle of a Cow

Domestic cows often give birth on a farm. Farmers often plan for births and look forward to adding to their herd. However, wise farmers know not to breed their cows until they are ready. Cows should not be mated until they are at least eighteen months old. When cows are pregnant, farmers feed them an especially *nutritious* mixture of grain and grasses. They usually give birth in the spring, and the calf has many warm months to grow strong. Cows can have one calf per year if they are chosen for breeding. In rare instances, twins are born.

Cows have a gestation period of nine months, just like human mothers. Newborn calves weigh about

Cows usually give birth to just one calf per year.

Once a cow is born on a farm, it is usually tagged early on so farmers can easily identify it.

100 pounds (45.4 kg). The farmer puts a tag on an ear of each new calf to identify it by number and to record its birth date.

Cows give birth in a calving pen separate from other areas of the barn. Pens provide a quiet place for the cow and her calf to recover from the birthing process. Once a calf is born, the mother cow uses her long tongue to lick her offspring clean. The calving pen is a safe place where the shaky newborn can grow until it is big enough to mingle with the herd.

A new calf can stand on wobbly legs almost immediately after being born. Hungry for milk, it instinctively searches under its mother's belly to suckle.

The cow's milk is full of nutrients to help the calf grow strong. It also helps protect the calf from sickness and disease.

If the mother is a dairy cow, the calf will be taken off its mother's milk after a few days. The dairy farmer needs to sell the milk she produces. The

Calves of dairy cows are bottle-fed by farmers so that its mother's milk can be sold.

Did You Know . . .

The oldest known cow was named Big Bertha. She lived to be forty-eight years old. Big Bertha also holds the record for producing the most offspring. She had thirty-nine calves during her lifetime.

farmer then hand-feeds the calf milk and, eventually, feeds it other foods. A calf born on a beef farm is usually allowed to drink milk from its mother for about six months.

At around one month of age, calves begin to eat a special mixture of grain. Soon they begin to eat *silage*, which is often corn and grass mixed together. In a few more weeks, they will eat other grasses and hay. Calves grow amazingly fast; they gain as much as a pound per day. By the time they are a year old, they weigh over 600 pounds (272 kg). At two years of age, they are considered fully grown. A grown cow can eat its weight in grass every week.

Breeding is very important for farmers. It not only adds new cows to their herd but also helps produce healthy cows. Selective breeding brings out the most desirable traits in cows, so that dairy cows produce more milk and beef cows produce more meat. It also makes cows more resistant to disease and more adaptable to harsh climates.

Straightbreeding involves mating within a specific breed—for example, mating a Guernsey with another Guernsey. This keeps the breed pure. Crossbreeding means mating a cow with a bull from a different

The Scottish Highland breed has long hair to keep it warm in the cold climates it populates.

breed—perhaps mating a Guernsey with a Brown Swiss. There are many breeding societies made up of groups of breeders who work to improve a certain breed. They keep herd books, which are records of all the animals registered in a given breed. When new calves are born, they are given a herd number. Breeders work hard to make sure their breed is desirable and high-performing.

4 Time to Eat

Cows require a lot of food. They also need plenty of water—about 15 gallons (57 liters) a day. Cows generally spend spring, summer, and fall grazing in pastures. When the cows eat all the grass in a particular pasture, the farmer moves them to a new pasture. In the winter, when grass is unavailable, the farmer moves the cows into the barn and feeds them silage, grains, and hay. The farmer carefully monitors how much food the cows get so they will be healthy.

A cow's digestive system is complex. Cows do not completely chew their food before swallowing. This form of half-chewing is the first step in the digestive process. Amazingly, a cow has no upper front teeth, just a hard pad. However, it does have thirty-two

Cattle can spend up to eight hours a day eating the grass in a field.

When the weather turns cold and fields are covered by snow, farmers feed their cattle indoors.

other teeth, in the upper back and lower jaws. Coincidentally, adult human beings also have thirty-two teeth.

Cows are *ruminants*. This means they chew *cud*, which is partially processed food. A cow typically spends eight hours a day grazing, eight hours chewing cud, and eight hours resting and sleeping.

Cows have four stomach compartments: the *rumen*, the *reticulum*, the *omasum*, and the *abomasum*. When a cow eats, the partially ground-up food is formed into a ball called a *bolus*. The bolus is mixed with saliva and swallowed. It stays in the first stomach compartment, the rumen, until the cow feels full. In the rumen, stomach juices soften the partially chewed food.

Next, food travels to the reticulum. There it is softened further and formed into small balls called cud. During the feeding process, cows periodically regurgitate their cud, chew it again for about a minute, and then swallow it.

A cow spends a good part of its day chewing its food.

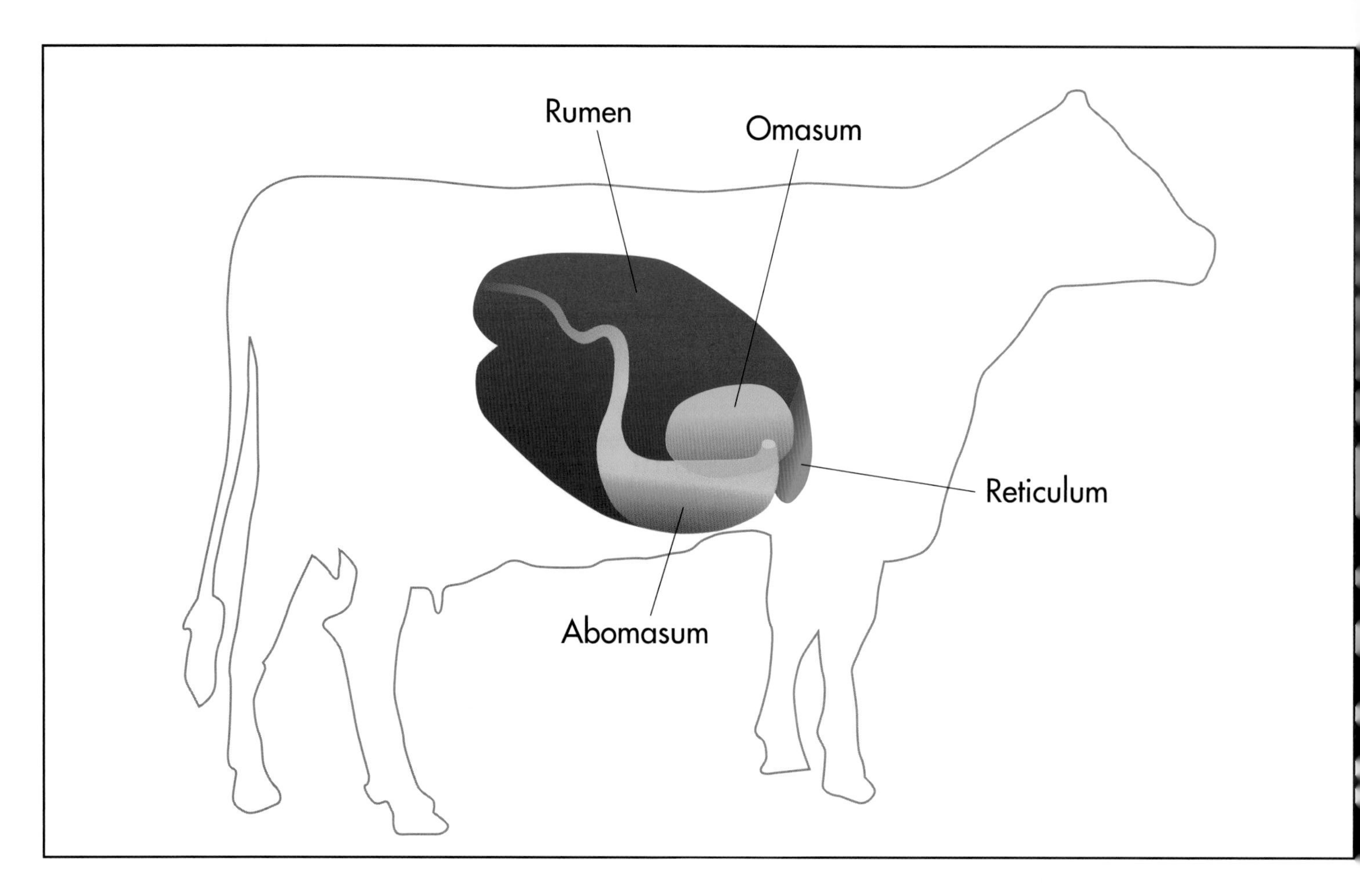

A cow has four stomachs, with each handling a different task.

Because a cow is continually eating or chewing cud, its stomach compartments always contain some partially digested food. The rumen and reticulum can hold 40 to 60 gallons (151 to 227 l)of liquid and food for several days. Microorganisms and various stomach acids begin to convert the food to nutrients for the cow.

The rechewed food then goes to the third compartment of the stomach, the omasum. This compartment acts as a filter, breaking down the food even further. In the omasum, water is absorbed from the food. The food is then ready for the final compartment, the abomasum.

The abomasum is the compartment most like a human stomach. This is where the digestive process is completed and food passes into the intestines. Any unused food turns into waste (manure). The food that a cow eats serves three purposes. It is processed into vital nutrients, it goes toward making milk, or it is made into manure.

Over half the food a cow eats is used for milk production. The volume and flavor of a cow's food affects the milk it produces. For example, a cow that eats a lot of sweet grasses produces sweeter tasting milk.

Because cows eat a great amount of food, they produce a great amount of waste. A mature beef cow produces about 65 pounds (30 kg) of manure per day. A dairy cow produces even more—about 1,500 pounds (680 kg) per day. Farmers do not waste the

Did You Know . . .

Cows are social animals that need to be part of a herd. They do not like to be alone. New cows introduced into a herd can cause a disturbance as they try to fit into established relationships. Cows often bellow if one of the herd is missing, and the separated cow bellows in answer to maintain contact with the herd. Herds are like big cow families.

This farmer stands near his flowing manure trough, which he uses to take his cow's manure and transform it into electricity, using a methane digester.

manure. They use it to *fertilize* their land. Manure contains many important nutrients, such as nitrogen, phosphorus, and potassium. These nutrients enrich the ground. Manure cannot be spread fresh. It is too strong and can harm plant growth. It is kept in a manure pile for several weeks or months and mixed with straw until it is ready for use.

Another byproduct of the cow's complex digestive system is *methane* gas. Cows *emit* this gas through burping and flatulence. Some scientists are concerned that methane gas from cows contributes to global warming. Fourteen percent of all methane gas emissions comes from farm animals, the majority of which are cows. Scientists claim that if the methane gas produced from one cow could be turned into usable energy, it would heat four households for an entire year. Methane digester machines, which convert the gas into electricity, are currently being used by some farmers.

5 Useful and Productive

Dairy cows are usually milked twice a day, once in the morning and once in the evening. The farmer leads the first cow toward the milking barn, and the others walk behind it. Cows are creatures of habit. They line up instinctively and stand in the same order almost every time.

Each cow is taken to a milking machine. A solution of iodine and water cleans the four teats. A rubber-lined cup is attached to each teat, and the machine pumps the milk out of the cow for about five minutes. This does not hurt the cow in any way. In fact, if the cow were not milked properly, her udders would become heavy and sore.

Dairy cows, such as those shown here, are usually miked twice a day.

Special machines now milk cows, even those living on small farms.

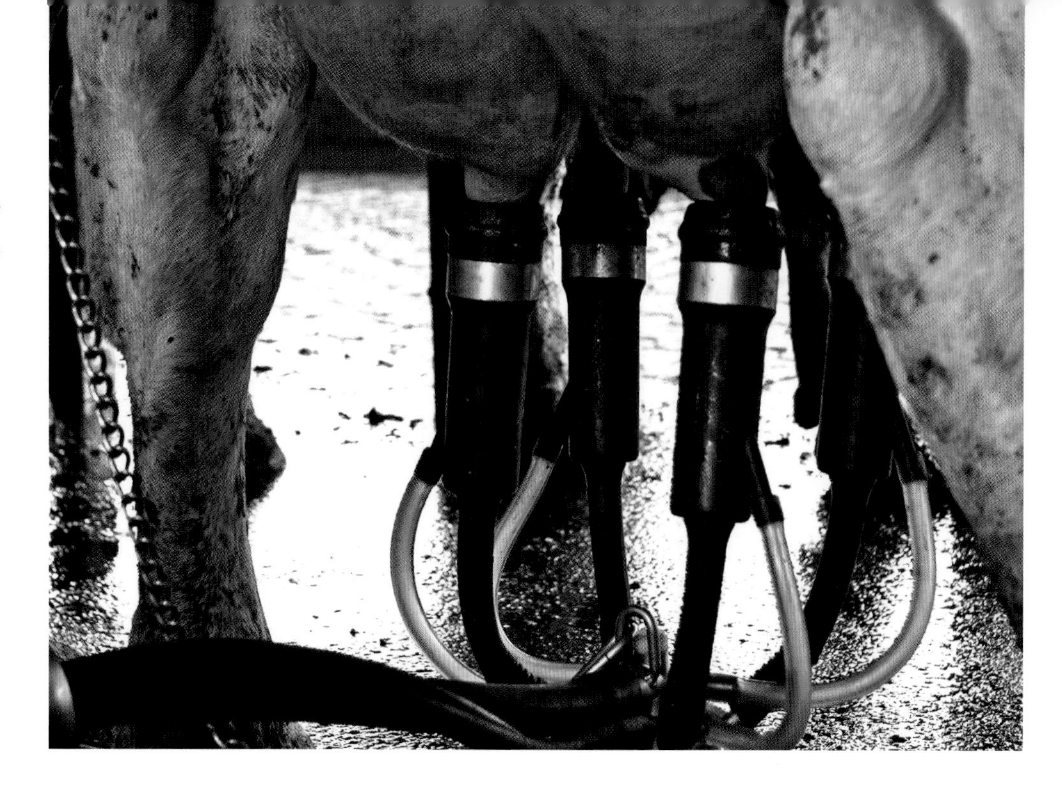

Dairy farmers rely on milking machines to make their farms efficient. It takes about one hour to milk six cows by hand. With a machine, the farmer can milk one hundred cows in an hour. Each cow is hooked to a machine for about five minutes. Cows each produce about 5 gallons (20 l) of milk per day.

After the milk is pumped, it travels through a pipeline to a cooling tank, which stores it at a temperature below 40 degrees Fahrenheit (4 degrees Celsius). Then it travels by truck to a dairy to be *standardized*, *pasteurized*, and *homogenized*. The milk is tested for butterfat content, flavor, odor, and the presence of *bacteria*. It is then moved to a clarifier, where it is cleaned and blended with milk from other farms. Now the milk has been standardized.

The next process, pasteurization, was invented by Louis Pasteur in 1862. The French scientist devised this method of heating milk to kill *viruses*, bacteria, and *mold*. Milk is heated to 165 degrees Fahrenheit (73.8 degrees Celsius) for sixteen seconds and then cooled. Pasteurization makes milk safer to drink.

During the final step, homogenization, milk is forced through tiny openings in a machine to break

In order to get milk into a typical grocery store, it must be pasteurized and homogenized by equipment like this.

Did You Know . . .

Pauline Wayne was the last family cow to live at the White House in Washington, D.C. She belonged to President William Howard Taft, who served from 1909 to 1913. Pauline Wayne often grazed on the front lawn of the White House and in the lawns of nearby public buildings.

Dairy cows graze on the fields of a farm in Wisconsin.

up fatty globules of cream. Once this process is completed, each drop of milk has the same amount of cream in it.

Dairy products are a big part of a well-balanced diet. People around the world enjoy milk, yogurt, ice cream, and cheese on a daily basis.

Beef products are also important to our diets as well as our economy. More than one million farms, ranches, and other businesses support the U.S. beef industry. About 800,000 ranchers maintain herds of various sizes. Most herds average about forty cows. The nation's cows produce about 27 to 30 billion pounds (12 to 14 billion kg) of beef per year—and the demand for beef continues to grow.

Even though the United States has less than 10 percent of the world's cattle, it produces 25 percent of the world's beef supply. This difference is partly due to excellent breeding methods, veterinary care, and improved feed.

A 1,000-pound steer produces about 430 pounds (195 kg) of beef. What happens to the remaining 570 pounds (260 kg) of bone, skin, and other body parts? Manufacturers make the hide into leather products such as clothing, shoes, luggage, upholstery, and sporting equipment. Intestines are turned into strings for musical instruments. Gelatin, which comes from connective tissue, is used in candy, jelly, and even marshmallows. Beef fat gets converted into engine oil and brake fluid. Other parts of a cow are used to make such diverse products as shaving cream, perfume, candles, detergents, wallpaper, and insecticides. Cows even contribute to important medicines like *insulin*.

Cows have been serving humans for thousands of years in many amazing ways. Even though we might not always think about it, most people drink, eat, and use products that come from cows every day. Cows are one of the world's most useful animals.

Glossary

abomasum—The fourth compartment of a cow's stomach, where the digestive process gets completed.

bacteria—Microscopic organisms, some of which produce disease.

bolus—A soft mass of chewed food.

branded—Put an identification mark on an animal by burning or freezing its flesh.

breed—A strain of related animals that humans create by mating domesticated species.

cud—Food that ruminants regurgitate to be chewed again.

domesticated—Made suitable for living near or with humans.

emit—To discharge into the air.

fertilize—To spread material that enriches land and helps plants grow.

graze—To feed on grass or pasture.

herd—A group of animals of one kind kept together.

homogenized—Processed milk to standardize the amount of cream present.

immigrant—One who comes from a foreign land to reside in a new place.

insulin—A hormone used to control a disease called diabetes.

methane—A colorless, odorless, flammable gas produced by the breakdown of organic materials.

migrate—To move from one country or place to another.

mold—A surface growth of fungus.

muzzle—The nose and jaws of an animal.

nutritious—Food that is nourishing and healthy for the body.

omasum—The third compartment of a cow's stomach, where water is absorbed.

pasteurized—Heated milk to kill viruses, bacteria, and mold.

reticulum—The second compartment of a cow's stomach, where cud is formed.

rumen—The first compartment of a cow's stomach, where stomach juices start to soften food.

ruminants—Animals that chew cud.

silage—Specially stored and preserved corn and grass that are used for animal feed.

species—A distinct group of animals that can reproduce together.

standardized—Cleaned and blended milk.

teats—The protuberances of the udder through which milk is drawn.

udder—A hanging sack in which milk is made and stored.

viruses—Infectious agents that can grow and multiply in living cells and cause disease.

Find Out More

Books

Donner, Andrea K. *Cow Tails & Trails*. Minocqua, WI: Willow Creek Press, 2005.

Stone, Lynn. *Cows Have Calves*. Mankato, MN: Compass Point Books, 2006.

Trumbauer, Lisa. *The Life Cycle of a Cow*. Mankato, MN: Capstone Press, 2006.

Web Sites

Did You Know?: Cow Facts
www.didyouknow.cd/cows.htm

Facts About Cows
http://aipl.arsusda.gov/kc/cowfacts.html

MooMilk
www.moomilk.com

Index

Page numbers in **bold** are illustrations.

About the Author

Renee C. Rebman has published more than a dozen nonfiction books for young readers. Her Marshall Cavendish titles include *Anteaters*, *Turtles and Tortoises*, and *Cats*. She is also a published playwright. Her plays have been produced in schools and community theatres across the country.